T0207920

Mutual Funds for Beginners

The Basic Guide You Need to Get
Started with Mutual Funds

Jason Fields

authorHOUSE®

AuthorHouse™
1663 Liberty Drive
Bloomington, IN 47403
www.authorhouse.com
Phone: 1 (800) 839-8640

© 2018 Jason Fields. All rights reserved.

No part of this book may be reproduced, stored in a retrieval system, or transmitted by any means without the written permission of the author.

Published by AuthorHouse 10/11/2018

ISBN: 978-1-5462-6388-3 (sc)
ISBN: 978-1-5462-6386-9 (hc)
ISBN: 978-1-5462-6387-6 (e)

Library of Congress Control Number: 2018912253

Print information available on the last page.

Any people depicted in stock imagery provided by Getty Images are models, and such images are being used for illustrative purposes only.
Certain stock imagery © Getty Images.

This book is printed on acid-free paper.

Because of the dynamic nature of the Internet, any web addresses or links contained in this book may have changed since publication and may no longer be valid. The views expressed in this work are solely those of the author and do not necessarily reflect the views of the publisher, and the publisher hereby disclaims any responsibility for them.

About the Author

Jason M. Fields, CFEI (Certified Financial Education Instructor). He holds a BS Degree in Business Management-Cardinal Stritch University.

Jason is the Managing Director of Dark Knight Capital Ventures and serves as the CEO/Ambassador of The Black Wealth Network. He is also the Co-Founder and Partner of DiversifyForex, a Foreign Currency, Stock, and Binary Options Investment Education Firm.

In 2005, Jason became the first African-American man to be elected to the Wisconsin State Assembly 11th District.

He is a published author having written two books.

He is currently working on his CHP (Certified Hedge Fund Professional) designation.

Jason started his career in the financial services sector where he helped actively manage over

$100 million in assets. His experience includes bonds, equities, derivatives, insurance, and residential and commercial loans.

He has been honored with several prestigious leadership awards, executive training and special designations, such as:

- *Governor Scott Walker Appointee to the Social Development Commission (SDC) 2012-Present*

- *The Bowhay Institute for Legislative Leadership Development, 2012*

- *Black Alliance for Educational Options 2012 Ed Reform Champion Under 40*

- *Hispanic Chamber of Commerce of WI, Government Advocacy Award, 2012*

- *Seat Belt Champion Award, 2010*

- *Wisconsin Minority Supplier Development Council Award for Excellence, 2009*

- *Ohio Coalition for Quality Education, Putting Kids 1st Award, 2008*

- *Specialized Medical Vehicle Association of WI Legislator of the Year Award 2008*

- *Wisconsin Builders Association, Friends of Housing 2007, 2008, 2009, 2010, 2011*

- *WI League of Conservation Voters, Conservation Champion 2008 & 2012*

- *Flemming Leadership Institute, Class of 2007*

- *Program for Emerging Political Leaders at the University of Virginia's Darden School of Business*

He is a member of Prince Hall Masons, Alpha Phi Alpha Fraternity, Incorporated, and The Independent Order of Odd Fellows.

The US Global Leadership Coalition and he is a member of the International Society of Business Leaders.

Jason is also a National Speaker on international business, financial literacy, and education reform policy.

Table of Contents

Introduction

The world of investing can come down heavily on you if you don't have a clear idea of what you are doing there. At one moment your investment might be touching the sky, and in the next, you might be thrown back down to earth.

Hence, learning the basics of the best investment for beginners can lead you to maximize your gains, as well as to minimize the possibilities of losses in the investment market.

If I could tell you what the best investments for beginners are every time, I would. The truth is, there are so many different determining factors mostly that are specific to you in this situation. What works great for one person may not work very well for another. I can, however, give you a few recommendations.

First of all, the amount of money you have to invest to make a big difference. For example, if you have $1000 to invest, you have much less to lose than a beginner who has $10,000 to invest. Of course, no matter how much you have to don't want to lose any.

As an absolute beginner, you should learn how to invest first, but at the same time, he should start investing right away. A great way to do this is to invest in mutual funds. What a mutual fund you can invest in virtually any investment without actually knowing how it's done.

MUTUAL FUNDS FOR BEGINNERS is designed to increase your awareness of the benefits of mutual funds and investing, and help you set realistic goals and expectations. If you would like to learn more, please visit our website at

https://www.thefinancialpromise.com.

Chapter 1

Introduction to Mutual Funds

Meaning Of Mutual Fund

Investing has become a big topic over recent months, and especially mutual funds have been shifted into the public spotlight. There seems to be a lot of confusion about these funds though, as many people do not seem to know what exactly mutual funds are or what they do. We will try our best to give you some insight and answer these questions.

Usually, when people talk about these funds, they are referring to a professionally managed collective investment scheme that is an amassment of money from a variety of investors which is invested into a verity of investment securities such as stocks, bonds, or commodities (mostly precious metals). Now, the big question is **what mutual fund is?**

Mutual funds are those professionally managed investment pools that, in a way, show the performance of several varied securities like stocks, bonds, and shares. An advisory firm usually organizes them to offer the fund's shareholders a specific investment goal.

With this, investors can buy shares of a mutual fund, for instance, the stock of a company. Anyone buying shares in the fund become a part owner and want to take part often because of those investment goals. To manage the company, the shareholders choose a board of directors to oversee the operations of the business and the portfolio.

Most of the time, the value of these mutual funds are calculated once a day, and that is based on what the fund's current net asset value is. For instance, a real estate mutual funds are one that invests in the real estate securities from around the world.

The real estate mutual funds usually tend to concentrate the investing strategy on the real estate investments trusts and real estate companies. These real estate investments trusts are mostly companies that purchase and manage real estate with help from the funds that were collected from the investors.

Mutual funds raise the money by selling shares of the fund to the public, much like any other company can sell its stock to the public. Funds then take the money they receive from the sale of their shares (along with any money made from previous investments) and use it to purchase various investment vehicles such as stocks, bonds, and money market instruments.

Most investors pick mutual funds based on recent fund performance, the suggestion of a friend, and the praise bestowed on them by a financial magazine or fund rating agency. While using these methods can lead one to select a quality fund, they can also lead you in the wrong direction and wondering what happened to that "great pick."

The history is a good indicator, though not a guarantee that a fund will do well. If you are investing long-term, the history will be of more importance than in a short-term situation as they say lightning rarely strikes the same place twice.

History of Mutual Funds

The first "pooling of money" for investments was done in 1774. After the 1772-1773 financial crisis, a Dutch merchant Adriaan van Ketwich invited investors to come together to form an investment trust. The goal of the trust was to lower risks involved in investing by providing diversification to the small investors. The funds invested in various European countries such as Austria, Denmark, and Spain. The investments were mainly in bonds, and equity formed a small portion. The trust was named Eendragt Maakt Magt, which meant "Unity Creates Strength."

The fund had many features that attracted investors:

- It had an embedded lottery.

- There was an assured 4% dividend, which was slightly less than the average rates prevalent at that time. Thus the interest income exceeded the required payouts, and the difference was converted to a cash reserve.

- The cash reserve was utilized to retire a few shares annually at 10% premium, and hence the remaining shares earned a higher interest. Thus the cash reserve kept increasing over time - further accelerating share redemption.

- The trust was to be dissolved at the end of 25 years, and the capital was to be divided among the remaining investors.

However, a war with England led to many bonds defaulting. Due to the decrease in investment income, share redemption was suspended in 1782, and later the interest payments were lowered too. The fund was no longer attractive for investors and faded away.

After evolving in Europe for a few years, the idea of mutual funds reached the US at the end of the nineteenth century. In the year 1893, the first closed-end fund was formed. It was named the "The Boston Personal Property Trust."

The Alexander Fund in Philadelphia was the first step towards open-end funds. It was established in 1907 and had new issues every six months. Investors were allowed to make redemptions.

The first true open-end fund was the Massachusetts Investors' Trust of Boston. Formed in the year 1924, it went public in 1928. 1928 also saw the emergence of first balanced fund - The Wellington Fund that invested in both stocks and bonds.

The concept of Index based funds was given by William Fouse and John McQuown of the Wells Fargo Bank in 1971. Based on their concept, John Bogle launched the first retail Index Fund in 1976. It was called the First Index Investment Trust. It is now known as the Vanguard 500 Index Fund. It crossed 100 billion dollars in assets in November 2000 and became the World's largest fund.

Today mutual funds have come a long way. Nearly one in two households in the US invests in mutual funds. The popularity of mutual funds is also soaring in developing economies. They have become the preferred investment route for many investors, who value the unique combination of diversification, low costs, and simplicity provided by the funds.

Structure of Mutual Funds

The mutual fund industry is highly regulated to imparting operational transparency and protecting the investor's interest. It is usually either a corporation or a business trust.

Like any corporation, a mutual fund is owned by its shareholders. Virtually all mutual funds are externally managed; they do not have employees of their own. Instead, their operations are conducted by affiliated organizations and independent contractors

How Mutual Funds Are Structured

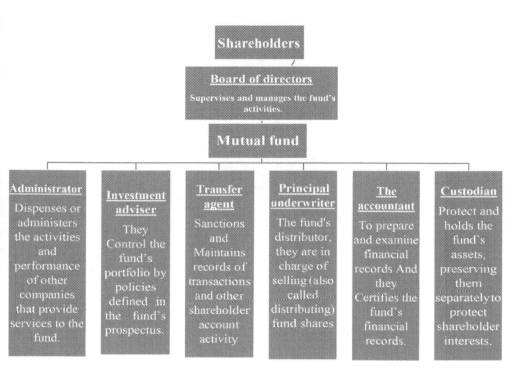

Shareholders

Board of directors
Supervises and manages the fund's activities.

Mutual fund

Administrator	**Investment adviser**	**Transfer agent**	**Principal underwriter**	**The accountant**	**Custodian**
Dispenses or administers the activities and performance of other companies that provide services to the fund.	They Control the fund's portfolio by policies defined in the fund's prospectus.	Sanctions and Maintains records of transactions and other shareholder account activity	The fund's distributor, they are in charge of selling (also called distributing) fund shares	To prepare and examine financial records And they Certifies the fund's financial records.	Protect and holds the fund's assets, preserving them separately to protect shareholder interests.

Chapter 2

Understanding The Types Of Mutual Funds

"If you don't act now while it's fresh in your mind, it will probably join the list of things you were always going to do but never quite got around to. Chances are you'll also miss some opportunities." - Paul Clitheroe

Types of Mutual fund

There are many different types of mutual funds for investors to choose from. No matter the type of investor that you are, you should be in a position to know the best options to fit your investment style. In America for instance, surveys indicate that there are more than 10,000 types of mutual funds for investors to choose from. This portrays that there are more mutual funds than stocks. With myriad options available and more to come for investors to choose from, choosing the right ones may turn out to be a daunting task. However, armed with all the necessary information, choosing the right investment option should be an unproblematic task.

It is imperative to understand that different types of mutual funds have different risks and rewards. Generally, the higher the potential return of investment, the higher the risk of loss. Though some may be riskier than others, all of them tend to have some form of risk. While you are investing, it is not possible to evade all the potential risks. Therefore, no matter the type of investment you are making, you have to be prepared for facing some risks only that some investments may be riskier than others.

All mutual funds usually have predetermined investment objectives. These objectives tailor the funds' assets, regions of investments and investment strategies. Generally, there are three main types of mutual funds, and they include; equity funds (stocks), fixed income funds (bonds) and money market funds. Usually, you are likely to come across the variations of these three classes of assets.

Let us have a succinct look at the type's mutual funds available;

1. **Equity Funds-** These are meant for investors, who are ready to take higher risk to maximize

return. These are also called stock funds. They predominantly invest in company stocks; therefore, they are characterized by high risk. It may invest in small, medium or large-cap companies, which is determined by the market capitalization of the company. Again, the portfolio manager may assume the different style of investment, i.e., value, growth or blend.

As the portfolio of these funds reflects the preponderance of company stocks, the return on equity funds largely depends on the stock market conditions. Capital appreciation in the long term is the primary objective of the stock funds.

2. **Fixed Income Fund-** FIFs are just the opposite of equity funds. Capital appreciation is not the focus of FIF. Here, security of the money invested assumes most of the importance. FIFs may invest in

different types of debt instruments like corporate, municipal and government bonds.

They may also invest in unconventional debt instruments like mortgage-backed securities. Retired persons can park their money here. Most of the fixed income funds prefer U.S. government bonds for investment because it has the highest credit quality. Instead of putting money in a fixed deposit, one should consider investing in fixed income funds.

3. **Money Market Fund-** The objective of an MMF is to give a safe investment option to the investor. Money market funds, primarily, invest in money market instruments. The portfolio of the fund contains cash equivalent short-term liquid assets.

The risk involved is very low for MMFs, and this is reflected in their low return profile. The good thing about these types of funds is that you can expect to get back twice what you would get from a savings account.

Apart from these three primary types, there are some other types of mutual funds.

Sector Fund: It targets a particular industrial sector to invest. For instance, you might fund sector funds that invest in just biotech, oil, and gas, electronics, or banking. Performance of these funds is highly depending on how well that industry is doing. They are more vulnerable to changes in a certain market sector than other funds, but also allow for significant profit from a sector that is doing well.

International Fund: IFs invest in international assets and companies. If you have heard, there are some great opportunities overseas; this might be a fund for you.

Value funds, on the other hand, invest in companies that the fund managers feel are undervalued by the market.

They may have had issues with management or a product, or maybe they are great companies, but most investors haven't picked up on them yet. These funds make a profit when their companies improve in either profitability or popularity.

Open Ended Fund: The fund house may issue and redeem fund units at any point in time depending on the demand for the fund.

Closed Ended Fund: Once issued the number of units cannot be increased later on by the fund managers. However, the units can be traded in a market at a premium or discount.

Index Fund: These funds create their portfolios keeping in mind the weight of different stocks in a benchmark index. Many index funds follow either S&P 500 or S&P CNX Nifty. The return on these funds almost exactly reflects the return of the benchmark index.

Growth Funds: Among the stock funds, the Growth fund is one of the most popular. This type of fund invests in growth stocks; stocks of companies who are developing new products and services, are in good financial order and are expected to grow faster than other similar companies in the market.

Chapter 3

Investing In Mutual Funds

Since you have never invested before, investing in mutual funds is a great opportunity and choice. As a first-time investor, you may be worried about choosing the wrong investments and losing money. You have to understand that any investment is a risk. You risk losing any or all of her money, but you could also make quite a bit of money. But more risk you take on, the more likely you will lose the money but also the more money you could make. You have to figure out the amount of risk you want to take.

Why Invest in Mutual Funds?

It is easy to understand why people would invest in mutual funds, but is it a smart play? I would say the majority of investors select mutual funds because

a)   *It is easy*

b)   *They think the professionals must be able to do better than them*

c)   *The only option in their company's 401K.*

Now there isn't anything you can do about a company not offering self-directed accounts, but most investors even given the option would go mutual funds over selecting stocks themselves. To compound the problem, the majority of investors select the top returning mutual funds from the previous year when they select one. If a mutual fund they own is doing bad, they will drop that one and take the highest returning fund in their pool of funds. Statistics prove that this strategy will not beat the S&P 500 over the long haul.

There is no doubt that their plenty of good mutual funds out there; in fact, there are some great ones. The problem is the majority of investors are not in these funds. I've read multiple articles with various stats on how many mutual funds beat the S&P 500 year over year. These numbers generally are between 10 and 20 percent, which is a staggering number if you think about it. Why would you want to park your money in a fund that isn't beating the indexes on a consistent basis? Why not just pick an index fund and avoid the fees.

Does anyone like paying fees? I know I don't and mutual funds charge you fees to run your account. They generally run between 1 and 2 percent, which may not sound like much but it can add up in a hurry. If you started with $10,000 and earned a compounded return rate of 7% in 20 years, it would be $38,697. Now let's say with that same starting figure you earn 8.5% (1.5% increase from above), your new total after 20 years would be $51,120. Now doesn't that extra money in your wallet/purse look nice just by avoiding fees!

If you have a fund that isn't performing well, we can assume the manager of the fund will likely swap in and out of winners and losers he or she is holding. They undoubtedly will not sit on their hands and watch their stock selections circle the drain. This movement in stocks is music to the ears of the brokerage firms that have their account. They are collecting transactions fees for every stock they get in and out of. Who do you think is paying for that?

Okay, this is all fine and excellent, but you don't have the time to pick stocks. It doesn't take as much time as you think with stock screeners and the amount of information on the internet these days. Now there are hundreds of different approaches to investing in stocks, so I won't get into which way is the best. You know your risk tolerance and can select stocks off that. If you don't trust yourself picking stocks, you can select stocks that the dependable investors like Warren Buffett or Carl Icahn select. You can even find several mutual funds that have historically beat the market over the years and look at their top 10 holdings. If they are in these stocks and have traditionally beat the major indexes, then they most likely are pretty good stocks.

The key to making your stock picks work for you is staying diversified. To what level of diversification should you have your portfolio setup? That again depends on your risk tolerance, but keeping your stocks spread out amongst the different sectors is a good way to avoid heavy losses. If you spent a little time researching stocks, you would see it is time well spent in most cases.

I know selecting stocks can be a scary process for a lot of people but at the very least aren't you better off in an index fund with no fees. When I am working on my portfolio, I have my best interest in mind, and I'm not sure that always happens when other people are playing with your money. As an exercise, it might be a good idea to write down stocks you are thinking of buying and track how they are doing compared to your mutual fund. What have you got to lose except the fees?

Tips for Investing in Mutual Funds

Before you invest, you need to do your research well. There are plenty of reputable mutual fund companies. You should study financial journals and websites before you shortlist some of them. Find out which funds have been performing consistently well.

You can ask for prospectus to find out how well the company has performed over both short and long-term. Compare the performance each year with the benchmark index. If the performance diverts from the index widely every year, it is probably best not to consider that company. Look for consistency rather than sudden peaks while choosing your mutual funds.

Another important point to consider when choosing your preferred investment is the objective of your investment. Depending on whether you are saving for your retirement or a college fund or a vacation, you can choose funds of varying levels of aggressiveness. Whatever the goal, decide what proportion of your portfolio should consist of mutual funds and stick to it.

You should always talk to the fund manager in question before you make a firm commitment. Once your decision is made, you should fill in all the forms properly. The great advantage of mutual funds is that once you have invested your time andeffort to search the company, you will have to devote little time to it. The fund will manage your investments, and you will enjoy a healthy profit.

Do Your Due Diligence before You Invest

When you have decided to invest, scrutinize the performance of the company. Perhaps its successes were achieved under a different management regime which has now changed. It is better not to change your stocks too often because every time you do so, a taxable return is generated. Finally, choose a no-load fund for your purposes. Do not forget to retain a copy of all your documents about mutual funds because you are going to need them for tax purposes.

Chapter 4

Buying Mutual Funds

As a beginner that's new to investment and you have decided that mutual funds are the way to go, the next logical question is how do you go about purchasing them? There are many different ways to go about investing in mutual funds, and you have several different options to choose from.

Before opting to invest in a fund, it is always better to know about different companies selling them and the fee they charge for their services.

Where to buy Mutual Funds

Insurance companies: Insurance companies should be the least considered option while buying a mutual fund. In most cases, insurance companies never sell this type of fund directly. They often combine the benefits of a mutual fund along with certain other products. These combinations are offered to customers in the form of unit-linked products. Another disadvantage of buying such products from an insurance company is the sales load that these funds carry. A sales load can be defined as the fund commission paid to brokers. This can range from 4 to 8 percent.

Banks: Another unfavorable place for buying a fund is a bank. Disadvantages of buying a fund from a bank are the same as they are with insurance companies. Even banks prefer to sell the funds in the form of loaded funds. Investors either need to bear the entry load or the exit load. Another disadvantage is that banks do not offer much variety keeping in consideration the investment objectives of the investor. Also, in most banks, no capable financial advisors are providing much information about the funds and their advantages to customers.

Stockbrokers and investment advisors: One should approach these groups with caution. Some of these people tend to sell the funds loaded with heavy entry or exit costs. Even if an investment advisor offers a no-load fund, he charges heavy fees for his financial service.

Discount stock brokers: These people are one good source of buying these types of funds. This is because these brokers are registered with different mutual fund companies and offer a wide variety of fund options to investors without any load. Discounted stock brokers are primarily preferred more than mutual fund companies due to their value of expertise in this sector, and also the advice they offer to customers are usually based on their investment needs.

Work's retirement program: Maybe the most common way of buying mutual funds is through your work's retirement program. Your 401(k) account is most likely tied to mutual funds so you may already be a seasoned mutual fund investor and not even know it. To find out more about the funds your retirement plan invests in, you can visit the website of the fund that your 401(k) invests in.

If you have signed up for a 529 College Saving Plan, then you've bought into mutual funds. These brand new plans are made for families who are trying to help their kids through college. Their main benefit is the tax laws that are used for withdrawals from the plan. In most cases, if money is taken out for education expenses, it's tax-free. This is an ideal plan for most families who are worrying about paying for college.

Mutual fund companies: These should be the most preferred source of buying a fund. It is one of the most popular ways to buy mutual funds is directly from the companies. The type of fund you want to look for is a no-load mutual fund. No-load funds are free from fees and additional costs that load funds tend to have. Since you're going directly through to the fund company, you will save a transaction fee that you would normally have to pay through a broker, and since you aren't paying any fees, all of your money goes towards investing.

Online: Another popular way to buy mutual funds is online through a broker or a mutual fund superstore. Most of these online superstores like T. Rowe Price or Wells Fargo (there are many others, as well) don't charge any transaction fees for their services because the fund you end up buying will reimburse them. Be careful though; these online superstores often sell funds that do carry transaction fees or them carry load mutual funds that can come with some steep fees of their own. Make sure you read all the fine print and know what you're investing in before you buy it.

Buying mutual funds in this day and age of the Internet is easier than it has ever been. But be careful, make sure you crunch the numbers and make an educated choice, and you can be well on your way to financial freedom with mutual funds!

Steps To Buying Mutual Funds

You can easily buy mutual funds for yourself. Following are a few simple steps for beginners.

1. Buy when a company makes their offerings to the public. During such a time, you will have to pay the face value instead of the market price, which also includes a premium in most cases.

2. You could buy the closed-end mutual funds, which are listed in the stock exchange, these help with trading purposes. These are normally at premium prices or according to the market demands

Here are a few things that are going to help you with buying.

1. You should decide on the money that you are ready to set aside to invest

2. You should decide if you are ready to wait until a new fund is being launched or you could buy at the IPO, you could also consider from a secondary market or directly from the company.

3. Normally funds of open-end have higher liquidity when compared to the funds that are the closed end; these have a very limited amount of shares. You could pick where you want to invest from them.

4. When you decide where you want to invest, you have the choice to pick out from different funds that also have the record of excellent performance.

5. Make sure you carefully go through the experience or history of mutual funds that you have short-listed.

6. You should check the mutual funds again that are invested in those stocks of any non-public companies. Companies that are non-public and

even others are not obligated to publish any financial result; therefore, you have no way of getting to know how your investment that is tied to companies has performed.

Chapter 5

The Pros And Cons Of
Mutual Fund Investing

Mutual funds have become an important aspect of the investment portfolio of many; this indicates they are proving to be beneficial to them. The gains one can expect from mutual fund investments no doubt they are promising, and there are other aspects too which make this option look lucrative.

However, financial experts believe that mutual funds have the edge over investments. Hence, it is important to understand the advantage of keeping an investment in a mutual fund.

The Advantages Of Mutual Fund Investing

Diversification: One of the greatest benefits of using mutual funds is investment diversification. When you invest in funds, you get a small piece of every stock, bond or international equity that your fund invests in. If you had to do this on your own, it would cost hundreds of thousands or even millions of dollars to participate. You get this diversification in every dollar you invest.

Low Initial Investment: Many funds have a minimum initial investment as low as $100 to $250. This allows nearly anyone to get started and gain exposure to the stock, bond, and international markets. There are two ways to begin investing in funds. You can open a Roth or regular IRA account for retirement, a non- qualified brokerage or mutual fund account and if you are serious... open both.

Professional Management: Let's face it, investing in the markets can be risky, especially when you are just starting and your experience is limited. Every mutual fund has a professional management team that has been buying and selling stocks and bonds for many years. When you invest in a mutual fund, you get their services as part of your investment. If you select a great fund with great management, you are sure to have great long-term results.

Liquidity: Having the ability to get your money quickly if you need it is another great benefit of mutual funds. If you place a trade order to sell (or buy) before 4:00 PM when the markets are open, your trade is guaranteed to be executed at the close of the market that same day. If you place it after 4:01 PM, your trade will be executed at the close of the next trading day. Having this guaranteed liquidity within a maximum of 24 hours is exclusive to mutual funds and adds a great deal of safety to your investment.

Concise information: Based on mandates from the Securities and Exchange Commission (SEC), fund companies are obligated to provide a simple, easy-to-understand prospectus and investor reports. A prospectus spells out a fund's goals, strategies, fees, and expenses. The shareholder report describes the fund's most recent performance.

Convenience: They provide a great deal of convenience for busy investors. Not only is it fairly easy to purchase fund shares, but they also offer automatic transfers and reinvestments of dividends and capital gains. You can also transfer your money from one fund to another.

Selection: There is a fund available for virtually any type of market sector that you might be interested in. A mutual fund screener is a good way to find high- quality funds for your portfolio. There are also mutual fund newsletters that provide investors with fund profiles and information.

Low Cost: There are many funds out there to choose from, so it is very important to find the best quality at the lowest cost possible. This usually means that you will invest in a "No-Load" mutual fund. No-load means you pay no commissions to purchase the fund, and 100% of your money go immediately into your investment account. You will also want to keep an eye on your mutual fund's annual expense ratio which is what the management team charges for their services. These can range anywhere from 0.5% to 1.5% depending on the type of fund that you invest in.

Return Potential: Probably the greatest benefit to investing in mutual funds is your potential to earn above-average investment returns. With bank savings accounts and CD's earning 1% to 3%, getting 6% to 10% annually over time from your fund will have a huge impact on the growth of your investment and the expansion of your wealth. Some mutual funds from the top management companies have even earned higher returns over a 10 and 15 year period. When you find these, hang on to them and enjoy the ride.

The Disadvantages of Mutual Fund Investing

No guarantee: As previously noted, mutual fund investors are not protected by any guarantees against losses in their fund investments. Stock funds invest in stocks, and the stock market rises and falls. Individual holdings within a fund and individual funds fluctuate in value.

Objectives: Several investment information companies categorize funds by their investment objective. Make sure that your fund manager invests according to the stated objective. Some funds drift away from their stated objective, and your money could be sitting idle as cash or being invested in different types of securities that the fund's objective states.

Diversification: Yes, diversification is both an advantage and disadvantage in mutual fund investing. Although investing in a large number of companies through a mutual fund can help insulate you from taking a huge loss in the stock market, it also prevents you from realizing a large gain that a smaller portfolio might realize.

Fees: Fees vary widely from fund to fund, and, in many cases, exceed the cost of employing a full-cost broker. Be aware of front-end sales charges, back-end sales charges, and ongoing operating expenses that cut into your returns.

Capital gains: Unless your investment is in a tax-sheltered account, you will be obligated to pay capital gains tax on the distributions you receive. By law, a fund's capital gains are passed on to shareholders, who must pay tax on them.

Final thought

Making your first investments can be tricky, expensive and risky. But if you choose a quality no-load mutual fund with a great management team, you should have a great start to your investment program. If you are unsure of what funds are best, make an appointment with a local "Fee-Only" financial adviser and let them help you get started. Either way, get started now. Your future and financial independence depend on it.

To sum up, mutual funds offer the investor large choices of various schemes with special features and can be chosen on the requirement of the investor.

Glossary of Investment Terms

#

Account Statement

A statement issued by a fund house providing the details of transactions and holdings of an investor in various schemes of the fund.

Annual Report

A report containing the yearly performance of the fund given to shareholders and investors.

Asset allocation

The allocation of total funds available in the portfolio in various asset classes like equity, debt, money market instruments etc.

Arbitrage

The purchase of an asset in one market along with a simultaneous sale of the same asset in a different market to take advantage of difference in price.

Automatic Reinvestment Plan

The option available to mutual fund shareholders wherein fund income and capital gains distribution are automatically used to buy new shares.

Asset Management Company

An organization appointed by the Trustees of the Mutual Fund, which takes investment decisions for the mutual fund and manages the assets of the fund.

Annuity

A series of periodic payments for a specific time frame.

B

Balanced fund

A fund that combines stocks, bonds and a money market component in a single portfolio.

Bond

A debt instrument that promises to pay interest and a fixed principal amount on maturity.

Benchmark

A standard against which the performance of a security or a mutual fund can be measured or compared.

Beta

A measure of the fund's volatility (systematic risk) in comparison to the market as a whole. Beta is used in the capital asset pricing model (CAPM) which calculates the expected return of an asset based on its beta and expected market returns.

C

Close-ended Scheme

A scheme that issues a fixed number of shares/ units for a specified period of maturity.

Corpus

The total amount of money invested by all the investors in a scheme.

Custodian

An organization, usually a bank that holds the securities and other assets of a mutual fund.

Compounding

Earnings on an investment's earnings. Over a period of time, compounding can produce significant growth in the value of the investment.

Capital Gain

The profit that is realized when the price of a security held by a mutual fund rises above its purchase price and the security is sold.

Commercial Paper

Short-term money-market instruments, issued by large, creditworthy corporates.

D

Debt Funds

A fund that invests in debt instruments like bonds and money market instruments.

Dividend

A portion of profit that a mutual fund distributes to its unit holders or shareholders.

Dividend Plan

A plan where the fund distributes its accumulated income from time to time as and when the dividend is declared.

Dividend Re-investment

A scheme where dividend from a particular investment is re-invested as opposed to being paid out.

Diversification

The practice of investing across a number of securities to reduce risk.

Dividend Distribution Tax

A tax payable by a debt-oriented mutual fund before dividend is distributed to the unit holders.

Dividend History

The track record of dividends declared by a fund.

Dividend Per Unit

Total amount of dividend declared by a fund for a scheme divided by total number of units issued to all the investors.

Dividend Plan

In a dividend plan, the fund distributes its accumulated income from time to time to the investors as and when the dividend is declared.

Dividend Reinvestment

In a dividend reinvestment plan, the dividend is reinvested in the scheme itself and is not paid out to the investors.

i.e. instead of receiving dividend in cash, the unit holders receive units allotted to them at the ex-dividend NAV.

Dividend Warrant

It is an instrument issued by companies/ mutual funds to an investor for the purpose of payment of dividends.

Dividend Yield

It refers to the dividend earned per unit of a scheme at the prevailing per unit price.

Dollar-cost averaging

Also known as Rupee-cost averaging. A practice where a fixed amount of money is invested at regular intervals regardless of whether the security prices are rising or declining.

Duration

Duration estimates how much a bond's price fluctuates with changes in comparable interest rates. If rates rise 1.00%, for example, a fund with 5-year duration is likely to lose about 5.00% of its value. Other factors also can influence a bond fund's performance and share price. A bond fund's actual performance may differ.

E

Equity funds

Funds that mainly invest in stocks i.e., equity (over 65% of its assets in equity stocks).

Exit Load

A fee charged by the fund when an investor redeems (sells) units from the fund.

Expense Ratio

The fund's cost of doing business as disclosed in the prospectus. It is expressed as a percentage of its assets.

F

Face Value

The original issue price of one unit of the scheme.

Fund Manager

An individual who makes all the decisions regarding investments of a mutual fund scheme.

Fund of funds

All-in-one funds that invest in other mutual funds.

G

Gilt Funds

Funds that mainly invest in government securities of different maturities.

Government Securities

Securities created and issued by the Government (Central/ State) that are sold to the public.

Growth Plans

A plan where the income earned is re-invested in the scheme. The main aim is on capital appreciation.

I

Income

Dividend short term & long term gains paid to a mutual fund investor.

Income Fund

A fund whose main objective is current income rather than growth of capital. These funds invest in fixed income securities that pay regular interest.

Index fund

A fund whose investment objective is to match the investment performance of a large group of publicly traded common stock represented in a stock market index.

Inflation

The rate at which the general level of prices for goods and services are rising.

Inflation risk

The risk that a segment of an investment returns may be eliminated by inflation.

Issue Date

The date on which a security is deemed to be issued or originated.

J

Junk Bond

A speculative bond with higher credit risk.

L

Liquid Fund

A fund that invests in short- term instruments like treasury bills, commercial paper and certificate of deposit with maturity less than 91 days.

Load

A charge by the fund when an investor buys or sells units in the fund.

Liquidity

The ease with which an investment can be bought or sold. A person should be able to buy or sell a liquid asset rapidly with no adverse price impact.

Lock-in-period

The time period during which the investment amount cannot be withdrawn from the scheme it is invested in.

M

Management fee

The amount paid by the fund to the asset manager for its services.

Maturity

The date on which the principal of a security becomes due and payable to the security holder.

Mutual fund

An investment company that pools money from investors and invests that money into a collection of securities which includes stocks, bonds, and money-market instruments as defined in the Scheme Information Document of the mutual fund.

Money Market Instruments

Instruments that include commercial paper, treasury bills, GOI securities(less than 365 days), certificate of deposit, etc.

Mortgage

A legal instrument given by a borrower to the lender entitling the lender to take over pledged property if conditions of the loan are not met.

N

Net Asset Value

The per share value of a mutual fund found by subtracting the funds liabilities from its assets and dividing by the number of shares outstanding.

No load fund

A fund that does not charge any load for buying or selling its units.

Net Assets

The total value of a fund's cash and securities less its liabilities or obligations.

O

Offer Document

The official document (Scheme Information Document / Statement of Additional Information) issued by mutual funds prior to the launch of a fund describing the features of the proposed fund to its potential investors. It contains information required by SEBI pertaining to issues such as investment objective and policies, services and fees.

Offer Price

The lowest price that a seller is willing to accept from a prospective buyer. In the case of a mutual fund with a sales charge, this price is the net asset value (NAV) plus the sales charge. In the case of no-load funds, it is the NAV. The price at which units can be bought from a fund.

Opportunity Risk

The risk that a better opportunity may present itself after you have already committed your money elsewhere.

Open-end Scheme

A scheme where purchase and sale of units is done on a continuous basis.

<u>P</u>

Portfolio

A collection of securities owned by a fund that may include stocks, bonds and money market instruments.

Purchase price

The price at which a mutual fund's units can be purchased. The asked or offering price means the current net asset value per unit.

R

Rate of Return

The total proceeds derived from the investment per rupee initially invested. Proceeds must be defined broadly to include both cash distributions and capital gains. The rate of return is expressed as a percentage.

Record Date

A cut-off date announced by the mutual fund, for corporate benefits like dividends, rights, bonus etc.

Redemption

Buying back or cancellation of the units by a fund on an on-going basis or on maturity of a scheme.

Redemption fee

A fee charged by a limited number of funds for redeeming, or buying back, fund units.

Redemption Price

The price at which a mutual fund's units are redeemed (bought back) by the fund. The redemption price is usually equal to the current NAV per unit.

Refund

The act of returning money to an investor by the fund. This could be on account of rejection of an application to subscribe units or in response to an application made by the investor to the fund to redeem units held by him.

Registrar/Transfer Agent

The institution or organization that maintains a registry of unit holders of a fund and their unit ownership.

Repurchase

Buying back/ cancellation of the units by a fund on an ongoing basis or for a specified period or on maturity of a scheme. The investor is paid a consideration linked to the NAV of the scheme

Repurchase Date /Period

In the case of close-ended schemes, the specified date on which or period during which the investor can redeem units held by him in the scheme before the maturity of the scheme.

Repurchase price

The price of a unit (net of exit load) that the fund offers the investor to redeem his investment.

Risk Adjusted Returns

The expected returns from an investment depend upon the risk involved in the investment. For the purpose of comparing returns from investments involving varying levels of risk, the returns are adjusted for the level of risk before comparison. Such returns (reduced for the level of risk involved) are called risk-adjusted returns.

Rupee Cost Averaging

An investment approach based on investing equivalent amount of money in a fund at regular intervals.

S

Sales price

The price at which mutual fund offers to sell its units to investors.

Sector Funds

A fund which invests only in stocks belonging to a specific sector. For example, IT, Pharma, Infrastructure etc.

Security

An instrument evidencing debt or equity in a common enterprise in which a person invests on the expectation of financial gain. The term includes notes, stocks, bonds, debentures or other forms of negotiable and non-negotiable evidences of indebtedness or ownership.

Sharpe Ratio

A risk-adjusted returns measures, used to normalize absolute returns generated by a fund. Mathematically, the ratio is measured by dividing the excess returns generated by a fund, arrived by subtracting risk free return from the fund's absolute return, with the volatility i.e., standard deviation, of the fund.

Spread

The difference between the rates at which money is deposited in a financial institution and the higher rates at which the money is lent out. Also, the difference between the bid and ask price for a security.

Shareholder

An investor who owns shares of a mutual fund.

Sponsor

The parent organization that contributes atleast 40% of the net worth of the asset management company (AMC).

Systematic Investment Plan (SIP)

A plan which enables an investor to have a designated sum of money transferred regularly from his or her bank account to the fund account.

Systematic Transfer Plan

A plan that allows the investor to give consent to the fund to periodically transfer a certain amount from one scheme to another.

Systematic Withdrawal Plan

A plan that allows an investor to withdraw a designated sum of money from the fund account.

Standard Deviation

A risk measure, which is used to determine the degree to which a fund's return fluctuates around its mean returns. It is also known as the volatility of the fund and is the most common risk measure used in arriving at risk-adjusted returns.

T

Tracking Error

The negative difference between the returns generated by a fund and the benchmark it tracks.

Trustee

Board of Trustees or the Trustee Company who hold the property of the Mutual Fund in trust for the benefit of the Unitholders.

Total Return

A measure of funds performance that includes all elements of return - dividends, capital gain distribution and changes in net asset value.

Transfer Agent

An organization appointed to prepare and maintain registry of unitholders of the fund and their unit ownership.

Turnover

Portfolio turnover is the rate at which a mutual fund manager buys or sells securities in a fund. A high turnover rate, which normally signals a strategy of capitalizing on opportunities to sell at a profit, has the potential downside of generating short-term capital gains. That means the gains are usually taxable as ordinary income rather than at the lower long-term capital gains rate. Rapid turnover may also generate higher trading costs, which can reduce the total return on a fund.

U

Unit

A measure indicating one share of the assets of that particular scheme.

Unit holder

A person who holds units in a fund or under any plan of the Scheme.

Underwriter

An organization that acts as the distributor of an initial offer share to broker/dealers and investors and undertakes to subscribe to any under-subscription of the offer.

V

Valuation

Calculation of the market value of the assets of a mutual fund scheme at any point of time.

Value Date

The date on which a foreign exchange transaction or a cash movement takes place. It can be used interchangeably with settlement date.

Value Stocks

Stocks that are considered to be undervalued based upon such ratios as price-to-book or price-to-earnings (P/E). These stocks generally have lower price-to-book and price-earnings ratios, higher dividend yields and lower forecasted growth rates than growth stocks.

Vertical Integration

This is where a company merges or takes over other companies in the same supply chain. If a shoe manufacturer, takes over his supplier it would be vertical integration.

Volatility

In investing, volatility refers to the ups and downs of the price of an investment. The greater the ups and downs, the more volatile the investment.

Voluntary Plan

A flexible plan for capital accumulation, involving no specified time frame or total sum to be invested.

Volatility Measures

Volatility measures the variability of historical returns. Relative Volatility, Beta, and R"2" compare a portfolio's total return to those of a relevant market, represented by the benchmark index. Standard Deviation is calculated independent of an index.

Withdrawal Plan

A service offered by mutual funds allowing shareholders to receive income or principal payments from their account at regular intervals.

Y

Yield Curve

A graph depicting the relationship at a given point in time between yield on a bond vis-�-vis the maturity of the bond. The yield curve is positive when long-term rates are higher than short-term rates and negative or inverted when the long-term rates are lower than the short-term rates.

Yield-to-maturity

The compounded annual total return expected on a bond investment if it is held to maturity. To realize this return, you must be able to reinvest each interest payment at a rate equal to the yield to maturity.

Yield

Rate of return on a security determined by its coupon and other features expressed as a percent and annualized.

Z

Zero Coupon bond

A bond where no periodic interest payment is made. These bonds are redeemed at face value at the maturity date.

Printed in the United States
By Bookmasters